THE LAOTIAN CIVIL WAR

THE INTRANSIGENCE OF GENERAL PHOUMI NOSAVAN AND

AMERICAN INTERVENTION IN THE FALL OF 1960

BY

JARRED BREAUX

Thesis prepared for the degree of Bachelor of Art, University of Louisiana at Lafayette

Advisor: Judith Gentry, *Department of History*

The anti-Communist Laotian Minister of Defense, General Phoumi Nosavan, had planned to take control of Laos since the Neutralist Captain Kong Le was able the overthrow the Rightist government on August 9, 1960. General Phoumi and his pro-Western, Rightist forces used aid sent from the United States, which was supposed to be used to defend Laos against the Communist Pathet Lao and the Viet Minh, to gain military strength in Savannakhet. General Phoumi eventually gained enough strength to attack and conquer Vientiane on December 17, 1960.

During the Laotian crisis from August to December 1960, the United States sent aid to General Phoumi's Rightist forces, who were in active rebellion against the Laotian Royal Government under the administration of the Neutralist Prime Minister Souvanna Phouma. The United States had no intention of allowing Laos to become a totally neutral state; it wanted a neutral government that favored the West. Since the 1950s, the United States paid for the entire Laotian military, including soldier's salaries, training, and supplies, to make Laos a buffer zone to protect Thailand from Communism. A Neutralist government would allow the Communist Pathet Lao to gain a share of the power in Laos, something the United States did not want. General Phoumi had no intention of ever working with Souvanna Phouma, even after he was offered the position of Deputy Prime Minister. In August 1960, the United States Department of State and the Department of Defense backed the Rightist faction; however, the United States Department of State decided two weeks later that it was in the best interest of the United States to cooperate with the Neutralist government established by Prime Minister

Souvanna Phoumi on August 17. However, King Savang Vathana and Prime Minister Souvanna Phouma attempted to establish a coalition, neutralist government, which included Pathet Lao. The United States Department of State attempted to negotiate with the Royal Laotian Government to prevent this, but the United States Department of Defense had started to mobilize General Phoumi's forces. By December 1960, all chances of Laos becoming a neutral nation were lost when General Phoumi seized control of the government.

In 1954, Laos was granted its complete independence from France. The Rightist pro-Western faction, the Leftist Communist faction (Pathet Lao), and the Neutralist in Laos established a Constitutional monarchy and worked together at first to establish a strong, neutral country. Limited in power, King Sisavang Vong rounded up support for Laos in the West. On December 13, 1955, the United States established the Programs Evaluations Office, an aid organization to help Laos stabilize its government and economy, in Vientiane. In reality, the Programs Evaluations Office was a secret United States military presence to establish Laos as a military power.

Cooperation between the factions in Laos continued until the February 1957 elections. In May of 1957, Prime Minister Souvanna Phouma resigned because of lack of cooperation by the Rightists. A pro-American government under Phoui Sananikone was established a month later. Souvanna Phouma returned as Prime Minister in August of 1957. King Sisavang Vong died in October of 1959, and General Phoumi Nosavan attempted to seize power in Laos in January of 1960. Persuaded by the United States to establish a democratic government, the new king, King Savang Vathana, appointed Kou Abhay set up a provisional government and appointed General Phoumi the office of Minister of Defense. General Phoumi Nosavan rigged the national elections in April 1960 to favor the Rightists. Tiao Samsanith, who was a puppet for General Phoumi Nosavan, was elected as Prime Minister. General Phoumi Nosavan was only partially successful in rigging the elections. Prince Souvanna Phouma, a Neutralist, won the election for president of the National Assembly even though General Phoumi Nosavan rigged the elections. Fighting between the factions commenced soon after the election results.[1]

On August 9, 1960, Captain Kong Le and his Neutralist battalion were able to seize control of the administrative capital of Vientiane, while Prime Minister Tiao Samsanith, government officials, and military leaders met in the royal capital of Luang Prabang. Immediately, Thailand imposed an embargo on the city of Vientiane. The United States Secretary of State, Christian Herter, made it clear that the United States supported the "legitimate government under the King's direction." The United States supported the pro-Western government of Prime Minister Tiao Samsanith, even though it was elected illegally. The Neutralist forces at Vientiane organized the Executive Committee of the High Command of the Revolution as the interim government in Laos the following day. General Phoumi Nosavan, stated on August 10 that he planned to retake Vientiane by

---

[1]David Wise and Thomas B. Ross, *The Invisible Government* (New York: Random House, 1964), 148-49; Edward Friedman and Mark Selden, *American's Asia: Dissenting Essays on Asian-American Relations* (New York: Random House, 1969), 267-79; and Alexander L. George, David K. Hall, and William E. Simons, *The Limits of Coercive Diplomacy: Laos, Cuba, Vietnam* (Boston, Mass.: Little, Brown, and Company, 1971), 36-39.

force. The United States Ambassador to Laos, Winthrop G. Brown, responded to General Phoumi by stating that the United States supported a restoration of peace "through quick and decisive action."[2]

The United States prepared to deal with the Laotian crisis militarily and politically in order to secure Laos from Communist takeover. The Department of Defense and the Department of State of the United States approved measures on August 12 to support the Royal Laotian Government at Luang Prabang and Savannakhet. The Department of Defense ordered two liaison officers of the Programs Evaluation Office to meet with Forces Armee Lao (the Laotian army) commanders, who were under the direction of General Phoumi, in Luang Prabang and Savannakhet. These officers supplied logistical support and intelligence to the Forces Armee Lao.

The United States Department of State and the Department of Defense did not always agree on how to handle the situation in Laos. When General Phoumi stated that he wanted to retake the capital city by force, the United States Department of State objected. The Commander in Chief Pacific supported General Phoumi's decision and called for the Joint Chiefs of Staff to back the Rightist forces with money and transportation. On August 19, 1960, the Secretary of Defense contacted the Secretary of State and asked for aircraft to

---

[2] Joint Chiefs of Staff, *Chronological Summary of Significant Events Concerning the Laotian Crisis, First Installment: 9 August 1960 to 31 January 1961* (Washington, D.C.: Historical Division, Joint Secretariat, 1961), 1; Australia, Department of External Affairs, *Selected Documents on International Affairs No. 16: Laos* (Canberra, Australia: W.G. Murry Government Printer, 1970), 72; Bernard Fall, *Anatomy of a Crisis: The Laotian Crisis of 1960-1961* (Garden City, N.Y.: Doubleday, 1969), 187-88; and Bill Lair, "Interview with Bill Lair," interviewed by Steve Maxner, transcript, 11 December 2001, Vietnam Archive at Texas Tech University, 95.

support General Phoumi. The United States Department of State granted Royal Laotian Government the use of supplies stockpiled in Thailand, which included the use of at least one aircraft. However, the United States ended up only sending aircraft for transportation of political dignitaries in order to negotiate peacefully.[3]

On August 13, 1960, the Laotian National Assembly in Vientiane, under influence of the Neutralists, called for a vote of no-confidence in Prime Minister Samsanith and nominated Prince Souvanna Phouma for the position of Prime Minister. Despite objections from the United States, Prime Minister Somsanith resigned on August 15. King Savang Vathana of Laos appointed Prince Souvanna as the new Prime Minister. The appointments of Prime Minister Souvanna Phouma were approved on August 17 by the National Assembly. General Phoumi did not accept the Neutralist government, but he opened negotiations with the Neutralists to stall their efforts.[4]

The Neutralist forces now controlled the Royal Laotian Government. Upset with the new appointments, General Phoumi formed the "Committee Against the Revolutionary Camp." It dropped leaflets from airplanes over Vientiane, which stated that its goal was to

---

[3] Joint Chiefs of Staff, *Chronological Summary*, 2-6; Lair, "Interview with Bill Lair," 95; and Major John C. Pratt, *The Royal Laotian Air Force 1954-1970* (Christiansburg, Va.: Dalley Book Service, 1994), 3-4.

[4] Joint Chiefs of Staff, *Chronological Summary*, 2-3; Fall, *Anatomy of a Crisis*, 188; and Arthur J. Dommen, *Conflict in Laos: The Politics of Neutralization* (New York: Praeger, 1971), 146-47; Charles A. Stevenson, *The End of Nowhere: American Policy Toward Laos Since* 1954 (Boston, Mass.: Beacon Press, 1972), 96; and Sisouk Na Champassak, *Storm Over Laos: A Contemporary* History (New York: Praeger, 1961), 158, 162-63.

reestablish order in Laos and accused Kong Le of "inviting" the Chinese into Laos and "forcing" Prime Minister Samsanith to resign.[5]

In an effort to ease tensions between the Neutralists and the Rightists, the United States Secretary of State ordered the Chief of the UN Mission to go to the royal palace in Luang Prabang and ask the King to use his influence to convince General Phoumi and Prime Minister Souvanna to work together. Instead of supporting the pro-Western Rightists, the United States decided it would be in its best interest for the Neutralists and the Rightists to work together. At the request of the King, Prime Minister Souvanna flew to Savannakhet to meet with General Phoumi Phoumi on August 23. The new Laotian Commander in Chief, General Ouane Rathikone, accompanied Prime Minister Souvanna and was the representative of Kong Le and the United States military. General Phoumi and Prime Minister Souvanna reached an agreement to negotiate peacefully. On August 29, 1960, the National Assembly met in Luang Prabang with thirty-four representatives of Prime Minister Souvanna's Neutralist forces from Vientiane and twenty-two representatives from General Phoumi's Rightist forces from Savannakhet. Both groups of representatives were made up of elected members of the National Assembly before Kong Le's coup and dignitaries in Laos. Both sides agreed to a compromise, and the National Assembly approved the new coalition government. In the agreement, General Phoumi was given the

---

[5] Joint Chiefs of Staff, *Chronological Summary*, 4; and Dommen, *Conflict in Laos*, 147-48.

positions of Deputy Prime Minister and Minister of the Interior.[6]

Fearful of assassination, General Phoumi returned to Savannakhet instead of taking his position as Deputy Prime Minister in Vientiane. Prime Minister Souvanna reassured the United States that he wanted General Phoumi to take his position in Vientiane. However, General Phoumi then insisted that General Bounleth would have to be appointed Commander-in-Chief before he would take his position as Deputy Prime Minister in Vientiane. The United States warned General Phoumi that if he did not take his position, the United States would not support him politically or militarily. On September 6, 1960, Prime Minister Souvanna decided that General Bounleth would become Deputy Chief of Staff and that Captain Kong Le's forces would continue to withdraw from Vientiane and no more troops would be allowed into Vientiane. Because of General Phoumi's persistence, Prime Minister Souvanna soon changed two earlier decisions. He allowed General Amkha Soukhavong to replace Captain Kong Le as Deputy Commander-in-Chief as well as allowed General Phoumi to take a paratroop battalion with him to Vientiane. General Phoumi still was not satisfied.[7]

General Phoumi did not want to compromise, but rather he had already negotiated with Prince Boun Oum to form a resistance. On September 10, 1960, the United States military attaché attempted to

[6] Joint Chiefs of Staff, *Chronological Summary*, 4-8; Fall, *Anatomy of a Crisis*, 190; Dommen, *Conflict in Laos*, 149-50; and Stevenson, *The End of Nowhere*, 97-98.

[7] Joint Chiefs of Staff, *Chronological Summary*, 8-14; Dommen, *Conflict in Laos*, 150-51; George, Hall, and Simons, *The Limits of Coercive Diplomacy*, 40; and Stevenson, *The End of Nowhere*, 99.

convince General Phoumi to go to Vientiane. Before the conclusion of the meeting, General Phoumi stated that a revolution against Prime Minister Souvanna would be announced shortly. The announcement from Savannakhet stated that Prince Boun Oum had "taken control" of Laos and "exiled" Prime Minister Souvanna from Laos to protect the country. Prince Boun Oum was not in the position to actually take over the country or to exile Prime Minister Souvanna; however, the announcement was the beginning of a rebellion against the Laotian Royal Government. Even though King Savang favored General Phoumi, he was powerless to act. King Savang stated that negotiation between Prime Minister Souvanna and General Phoumi would not work at this point. On September 16, 1960, the United States Acting Secretary of State made it clear that the United States would not support the insurrection of Prince Boun Oum and General Phoumi. The United States would also not fully support Prime Minister Souvanna and suggested new negotiations in the royal capital of Luang Prabang. Prime Minister Souvanna stated that he would like to resume negotiations with General Phoumi and that he would retire if King Savang asked. On September 22, 1960, King Savang agreed to resume talks as soon as fighting, which had erupted between the Rightists, the Neutralists, and the Leftists six days before, had stopped. King Savang decided that Souvanna would remain as Prime Minister and General Phoumi would be appointed as Commander-in-Chief. Still dissatisfied, General Phoumi claimed that Luang Prabang was unsafe and suggested that King Savang assume direct control of Laos.[8]

---

[8] Joint Chiefs of Staff, *Chronological Summary*, 14-21; Fall, *Anatomy of a Crisis*, 190-92; Dommen, *Conflict in Laos*, 154; and Department of External Affairs,

While Prime Minister Souvanna was attempting to reach a compromise with the factions in Laos, the forces of General Phoumi, Prime Minister Souvanna and the Pathet Lao engaged each other on the battlefield. On September 16, 1960, the Pathet Lao attacked General Phoumi's army in Sam Neua. The United States military sent military supplies from Thailand to General Phoumi's forces in Sam Neua. The United States officially stated that its aid was not politically motivated but rather to secure Laos. The next day, Prime Minister Souvanna confirmed that the Pathet Lao attacked General Phoumi's army for being loyal to Prince Boun Oum. Prime Minister Souvanna also pointed out that the Rightist forces of General Phoumi were in active rebellion against the Laotian Royal Government. On September 20, 1960, the Pathet Lao ceased military operations in Sam Neua and agreed to support Prime Minister Souvanna. However, that same day, Prime Minister Souvanna's forces, under the leadership of Captain Kong Le, started fighting with General Phoumi's forces in Paksane. On September 26, 1960, the Pathet Lao again attacked General Phoumi's forces. This time, General Phoumi and Prime Minister Souvanna stopped fighting each other in order to combat the Pathet Lao together. By the beginning of October, military operations had stopped and negotiations between the factions resumed. The battles were nothing more than skirmishes, and there was no real gain of territory of strategic importance nor was there a significant loss on either side.[9]

Since the beginning of the crisis there was always a question of whether or not United States would continue to send aid to Laos. The United States paid for the entire Laotian military in order to combat the Communist Pathet Lao. When Prime Minister Souvanna and King Savang Vathana decided to open negotiations with the Pathet Lao, the United States expressed concern that aid sent to Laos could be used against the anti-Communist forces in Laos. On September 23, 1960, the United States Department of Defense suggested to the United States Department of State to discontinue aid to Laos defeat the Pathet Lao until its government became favorable with the United States. The United States Department of Defense wanted a Rightist government in Laos. The Neutralist government of Prime Minister Souvanna advocated equal representation of all factions in the National Assembly.[10]

Prime Minister Souvanna wanted to set up a coalition government, which would include all parties in Laos. The United States did not favor this proposal and continued the attempt to undermine Prime Minister Souvanna's power as it had in the beginning. Instead, the United States wanted Laos under the rule of a pro-Western leader who could unite the anti-Communist powers in

---

[9] Joint Chiefs of Staff, *Chronological Summary*, 17-22; Fall, *Anatomy of a Crisis*, 191; Dommen, *Conflict in Laos*, 154; and Toby Sisouphanh Panyanouvong, interview by author, tape recording, New Iberia, La., 1 March 2006.

[10] Ibid., 19-22; and Fall, *Anatomy of a Crisis*, 192; Goldstein, *American Policy Toward Laos*, 209-10; and Panyanouvong, interview by author.

Laos.[11]

By the end of September, it became clear that the Neutralist forces of Prime Minister Souvanna and the Rightist forces of General Phoumi were not going to work together. There was no one who could assume the office of Prime Minister and enforce compromise between the Neutralists and the Rightists. On September 18, 1960, Ambassador Brown stated that he saw no "respected figure" who could control the country and would not be considered a Rightist or Western "stooge."[12]

The world powers began to discuss who they wanted to have the job of Prime Minister. The British suggested on September 28 that Phoui Sananikone, the former pro-Western Prime Minister, was a good choice for Prime Minister. The French supported Prime Minister Souvanna Phouma over General Phoumi, since Souvanna had obtained power legally. The French commented that the United States and Britain should just accept Souvanna as Prime Minister since there was no alternative.[13]

Prime Minister Souvanna also opened negotiations with the Pathet Lao, and the government of Laos accepted the Neo Lao Hak Sat as an equal participant in a coalition government. By September 29, 1960, Prime Minister Souvanna had opened up talks with the Soviet Union. The United States threatened to no longer pay for the Laotian

---

[11] Martin E. Goldstein, *American Policy Toward Laos* (Cranbury, N.J.: Associated University Pressed, 1973), 211-10.

[12] Joint Chiefs of Staff, *Chronological Summary*, 18-22; Dommen, *Conflict in Laos*, 156; and Fall, *Anatomy of a Crisis*, 191-92.

[13] Joint Chiefs of Staff, *Chronological Summary*, 24-25.

military if King Savang Vathana did not assume control or appoint someone who could unite the military. However, King Savang Vathana initiated his own talks with the Soviet Union on October 5. The next day, the United States made the decision to discontinue aid immediately to Laos. A few days later, the United States decided to make one last plea to King Savang Vathana to end all talks with Communists. Most importantly, the King would have to end talks with the Pathet Lao. The United States Secretary of State ordered Ambassador Brown on October 18 to "sabotage" negotiations between Prime Minister Souvanna and the Pathet Lao.[14]

The United States became frustrated with the decisions of Prime Minister Souvanna and King Savang Vathana to negotiate with Communists. On October 7, 1960, the United States Ambassador in Thailand suggested that the United States should aid General Phoumi covertly. The United States knew it would be breaking the 1954 Geneva Accords, which the United States swore to abide by, by aiding the rebel forces of General Phoumi. The next day, the United States ordered the Programs Evaluation Office to establish permanent relations with General Phoumi and to transport military supplies to General Phoumi's Rightist forces. Officers of the Programs Evaluation Office would be assigned to advise General Phoumi's military; however, they would not be allowed to fight.[15]

On October 16, Assistant Secretary of State of East Asian and

---

[14] Toye, *Laos: Buffer State or Battleground,* 152; Joint Chiefs of Staff, *Chronological Summary*, 23-29, 33-35, 40; Fall, *Anatomy of a Crisis*, 193; and Dommen, *Conflict in Laos*, 159.

[15] Toye, *Laos: Buffer State or Battleground,* 153; Joint Chiefs of Staff, *Chronological Summary*, 29; and Fall, *Anatomy of a Crisis*, 193.

Pacific Affairs, J. Graham Parsons, reported that General Phoumi's Rightists forces had performed poorly in combat. He believed that the Communist forces in Laos could expose the aid being sent to General Phoumi covertly at any time and proposed the immediate cessation of aid to General Phoumi. In order to avoid such a disaster, Ambassador Brown negotiated with Prime Minister Souvanna for the equal distribution of aid to the entire Laotian military, both the Neutralist and the Rightist forces. However, Prime Minister Souvanna would agree only if General Phoumi would acknowledge the Neutralist government of Prime Minister Souvanna and dissolve the Revolutionary Committee. General Phoumi would receive direct military aid from the United States but would receive his pay from the government of Laos, once Prime Minister Souvanna had agreed to distribute aid equally. Prime Minister Souvanna anxiously awaited General Phoumi's messengers to receive the pay for General Phoumi's soldiers, but they never arrived. Believing that his messengers would be arrested for treason as soon as they entered Vientiane, General Phoumi absolutely refused to send messengers to Vientiane. The United States decided to continue to aid General Phoumi covertly.[16]

Ever since Kong Le's Neutralist forces seized Vientiane, General Phoumi had been devising a plan to take the city back. During a meeting on October 18, 1960, General Phoumi informed Assistant Secretary of Defense John N. Irwin II and Vice Admiral Herbert D. Riley that he planned to retake Vientiane by force. Instead

---

[16] Joint Chiefs of Staff, *Chronological Summary*, 31-33, 37-39; and Dommen, *Conflict in Laos*, 159-60; and Wise and Thomas, *The Invisible Government*, 150.

of rejecting to the idea, Assistant Secretary Irwin and Vice Admiral Riley told General Phoumi that he should plan the invasion for a later date. Assistant Secretary Irwin insisted to the Department of State that the United States give General Phoumi more covert support by assigning more American, Thai, and Vietnamese advisers to his army.[17]

The United States did not want Laos negotiating with any Communist country and expressed objections against Prime Minister Souvanna Phouma for collaborating with the Soviet Union. The United States became concerned that Laos might accept aid from the Soviet Union. The Laotian Royal Government had begun deficit spending, which was dangerous to the stability of the economy. Also, the embargo raised by Thailand since August 9 forced Laos to import goods through Cambodia, which was very difficult. On October 26, 1960, Prime Minister Souvanna told Ambassador Brown that he would have to take the offer of aid from the Soviet Union unless Thailand removed its embargo on Laos. Thailand quickly dropped the embargo the next day. The United States at least avoided Laos negotiating with the Soviet Union for aid, which could have ended up in the hands of the Pathet Lao. Since the Pathet Lao was a Communist organization, the Soviet Union would have probably supplied them with arms as well.[18]

On October 27, 1960, negotiations between Prime Minister

---

[17] Joint Chiefs of Staff, *Chronological Summary*, 34; and Goldstein, *American Policy Toward Laos*, 214.

[18] Joint Chiefs of Staff, *Chronological Summary*, 22-24, 27; and Dommen, *Conflict in Laos*, 156; and Fall, *Anatomy of a Crisis*, 195.

Souvanna and General Phoumi dissolved because General Phoumi was unwilling to compromise. Prime Minister Souvanna agreed to allow General Phoumi's representatives in the National Assembly only if the Neo Lao Hak Sat, political representatives of the Pathet Lao, was allowed as well. General Phoumi and the United States rejected the idea of allowing equal representation of the Pathet Lao in the Assembly.[19]

On October 28, 1960, the United States Department of State decided to persuade the King to advise Prime Minister Souvanna to resign. At this point, the United States advocated Phoui Sananikone for Prime Minister, despite objections made by Ambassador Brown. The United States and Britain believed Phoui Sananikone was someone who would form a government with Phoumi Nosavan and Souvanna Phouma, would support the United States, and was committed to forming a neutral Laos, that favored the west.[20]

The United States Secretary of State explained the best course of action was to again support a compromise between Prime Minister Souvanna and General Phoumi, which would allow the anti-Communists forces in Laos to unify. The Secretary of State persuaded Ambassador Brown to accept that Phoui Sananikone was the best choice for Prime Minister. United States Secretary of State and Ambassador Brown then devised a plan to make Phoui Sananikone the obvious choice for Prime Minister of Laos. Ambassador Brown approached Phoui Sananikone, General Phoumi, and Prime Minister

---

[19] Ibid., 37-38.

[20] Ibid., 38-39.

Souvanna separately to prepare them for a debate before the National Assembly. Ambassador Brown made it clear to Phoui Sananikone that United States' promotion of him as Prime Minister would be covert. Ambassador Brown confronted Prime Minister Souvanna about his earlier decision to allow the Neo Lao Hak Sat in the executive cabinet. Ambassador Brown also questioned Prime Minister Souvanna's appointments to the National Neutrality and Unity Committee, since on October 31, Kong Le was appointed as an officer. Ambassador Brown informed General Phoumi that it would be in his best interest if he would open negotiations with Phoui Sananikone. The United States Secretary of State ordered Ambassador Brown not to reveal United States' support of Phoui Sananikone as Prime Minister to General Phoumi. Even though the United States carefully prepared all three sides for the conference, the debate never took place. On November 16, 1960, King Savang Vathana made it clear that he would not agree to allow an open debate before the National Assembly.[21]

While the United States was advocating Phoui Sananikone for Prime Minister, Luang Prabang came under the control of General Phoumi. Major Baunpheun Isixiengmay, commander of the garrison in Luang Prabang, shifted his allegiance from Kong Le and Prime Minister Souvanna to General Phoumi on November 11, 1960. Because Major Baunpheun had defected from Kong Le's command, the Joint Chiefs of Staff feared an attack by Kong Le and ordered the Commander-in-Chief Pacific to deny Kong Le access to American aircraft in Laos. On November 14, 1960, Prime Minister Souvanna

---

[21] Ibid., 40-42.

devised a plan for his remaining military forces to attack Luang Prabang. Since General Phoumi completely refused to negotiate, Prime Minister Souvanna decided to make an example of General Phoumi in order to demonstrate the authority of the Royal Laotian Government. Ambassador Brown informed the United States Secretary of State in Washington that they would have no choice but to openly support General Phoumi if Prime Minister Souvanna attacked Luang Prabang.[22]

General Phoumi by then was in position to attack Vientiane. General Phoumi had the royal capital of Luang Prabang within his territory and Vientiane was cut off from supplies since Thailand had raised the embargo on Laos once again. The United States instructed General Phoumi to attack Vientiane only if the Pathet Lao attacked first. On November 17, 1960, another Neutralist commander from Prime Minister Souvanna's Neutralist forces, General Ouane Rathikone, defected and pledged his support for General Phoumi, which gave General Phoumi the advantage he needed to conquer Vientiane.[23]

General Phoumi only needed the United States to remove aid restrictions, such as the use of aircraft and weapons, in order to capture Vientiane. The Joint Chiefs of Staff lifted all restrictions on aid to General Phoumi on November 21, 1960; however, two days later, the United States abruptly stopped sending aid to General Phoumi. The United States Department of State reinstated the restrictions on

---

[22] Joint Chiefs of Staff, *Chronological Summary*, 43-44.

[23] Ibid., 43.

General Phoumi's forces in hopes of preventing all out war.[24]

In reaction to the defections, Prime Minister Souvanna announced a cease-fire between the Royal Laotian Government and the Pathet Lao. Prime Minister Souvanna stated that he would again attempt to form a coalition government with representatives from both the Neo Lao Hak Sat and General Phoumi. Prime Minister Souvanna requested a meeting in Luang Prabang with Prince Souphanouvong of the Pathet Lao and Prince Boun Oum and General Phoumi of the Rightist factions. A United States' mission traveled to Luang Prabang on November 24, 1960, to ask King Savang Vathana to allow the convention but he rejected the proposal two days later. Again, King Savang Vathana refused to allow negotiations between factions.[25]

Prime Minister Souvanna sent a representative to Savannakhet to speak with General Phoumi. Prime Minister Souvanna told Ambassador Brown that his representative had returned with "encouraging results." Supposedly, General Phoumi agreed that a coalition government, which included the Neo Lao Hak Sat, was the only way to bring unity in Laos. The Prime Minister's representative invited General Phoumi and his representatives to attend a conference in Vientiane, since King Savang Vathana had refused to host the negotiations in Luang Prabang.[26]

The negotiations in Vientiane would never take place either. In

---

[24] Ibid., 44; Panyanouvong, interview by author; and Friedman and Selden, *American's Asia*, 284.

[25] Ibid., 42-47; Department of External Affairs, *Selected Documents on Laos*, 74-75; Dommen, *Conflict in Laos*, 161-64; Fall, *Anatomy of a* Crisis, 195-96.

[26] Joint Chiefs of Staff, *Chronological Summary*, 48.

preparation for a planned siege of Luang Prabang, Prime Minister Souvanna moved his troops on November 25 from the administrative capital of Vientiane to approximately sixty-five miles south of Luang Prabang. The next day, they began the march to Luang Prabang. However, along the way, many of Prime Minister Souvanna's forces abandoned the march to join General Phoumi's side.[27]

Meanwhile, General Phoumi's forces held their position in Luang Prabang. The Department of State and the Department of Defense both agreed that restrictions on General Phoumi should remain in place until Prime Minister Souvanna's forces or the Pathet Lao attacked. Because Luang Prabang was in imminent danger, the Commander-in-Chief Pacific once again asked the Joint Chiefs of Staff on December 4 to lift the restrictions on General Phoumi. The restrictions were finally lifted on December 6, despite there having been no attack against General Phoumi.[28]

With restrictions lifted and the majority of Neutralist forces having left Vientiane to attack Luang Prabang, General Phoumi could then take over the city of Vientiane. December 7, 1960, a supporter of General Phoumi embedded in Souvanna's Neutralist forces, Colonel Kouprasith Abhay, revealed to Ambassador Brown a new plan to overthrow Souvanna's government. That same day, General Phoumi's forces began their march toward Vientiane. Colonel Kouprasith deceived Prime Minister Souvanna into believing that General Phoumi's forces were there to support him against the Communists.

---

[27] Joint Chiefs of Staff, *Chronological Summary,* 46-48; and Fall, *Anatomy of a Crisis*, 197

[28] Joint Chiefs of Staff, *Chronological Summary*, 48-50.

The coup d'etat began during the early morning hours of December 8, 1960. Kong Le discovered Colonel Kouprasith's deception and seized the important parts of the city on December 9. When Prime Minister Souvanna figured out that General Phoumi's forces had come to take over the city, he fled to Cambodia. Quinim Polsena, the Leftist Minister of Information, declared himself Prime Minister on December 11, 1960. The next day, General Phoumi led the Laotian National Assembly into session in Savannakhet and elected General Phoumi's Revolutionary Committee to form the Provisional Government of Laos. Nevertheless, by December 17, General Phoumi had complete control over Vientiane.[29]

---

[29] Ibid., 51-58; Goldstein, *American Policy Toward Laos*, 217-18; Department of External Affairs, *Selected Documents on Laos*, 75-79; Fall, *Anatomy of a Crisis*, 197-99; Dommen, *Conflict in Laos*, 164-70; Thomas, *The Invisible Government*, 150-51; and Panyanouvong, interview by author.

WORKS CITED

Primary Sources

Adams, Nina S., and Alfred W. McCoy, eds. *Laos: War and Revolution.* New York: Harper Colophon Books, 1970.

Andelman, David A. "Laos Falls to the Communists: I Was There." *American Heritage Magazine,* 2 December 2005. American Heritage. http://www.americanheritage.com/articles/web/20051202-communism-catfish-vietnam-thailand-cambodia-pathet-lao-cia-bangkok-vientiane.shtml.

Australia. Department of External Affairs. *Select Documents on International Affairs No. 16: Laos.* Canberra, Australia: W. G. Murray Government Printer, 1970.

Champassak, Sisouk Na. *Storm over Laos: A Contemporary History.* New York: Praeger, 1961.

Chomsky, Noam. "A Special Supplement: A Visit to Laos." *New York Review of Books* 15:2, 23 July 1970. New York Review of Books. http://www.nybooks.com/articles/10894.

Fall, Bernard. *Anatomy of a Crisis: The Laotian Crisis of 1960-1961.* New York: Doubleday, 1969.

Joint Chiefs of Staff. *Chronological Summary of Significant Events concerning the Laotian Crisis, First Installment: 9 August 1960 to 31 January 1961.* Washington, D.C.: Historical Division, Joint Secretariat, 1961.

_____. *Chronological Summary of Significant Events concerning the Laotian Crisis, Second Installment: 1 February to 31 March 1961.* Washington, D.C.: Historical Division, Joint Secretariat, 1961.

_____. *Chronological Summary of Significant Events concerning the Laotian Crisis, Third Installment: 1 April to 31 May 1961*. Washington, D.C.: Historical Division, Joint Secretariat, 1961.

_____. *Chronological Summary of Significant Events concerning the Laotian Crisis, Fourth Installment: 1 June to 31 December 1961*. Washington, D.C.: Historical Division, Joint Secretariat, 1962.

_____. *Chronological Summary of Significant Events concerning the Laotian Crisis, Fifth Installment: 1 January to 30 April 1962*. Washington, D.C.: Historical Division, Joint Secretariat, 1962

Lair, Bill. "Interview with Bill Lair." Interviewed by Steve Maxner, 11 December 2001. Vietnam Archive at Texas Tech University. http://www.vietnam.ttu.edu/star/images/oh/oh0200/OH0200-part1.pdf.

Laos. Ministry of Foreign Affairs of Laos. *White Book on the Violations of the Geneva Accords of 1962 by the Government of North Vietnam*. Vientiane, Laos: Ministry of Foreign Affairs of Laos, 1968.

Panyanouvong, Toby Sisouphanh, son of military commander Lith Panyanouvong. Interview by author, 1 March 2006, New Iberia, La. Tape recording. University of Louisiana, Lafayette, La.

Sananikone, Brigadier General Oudone. "Civic Action in Laos: 1957-1959." *Current Civil Affairs Trends* 13 (September 1963): 3-24.

_____. *The Royal Lao Army and U.S. Army advice and support*. Washington, D.C.: U.S. Army Center of Military History, 1981.

Shaplen, Robert. *A Turning Wheel: Three Decades of the Asian Revolution as Witnessed by a Correspondent for The New Yorker*. New York: Random House, 1979.

U.S. Congress. Senate. Committee on Appropriations. *A Report of United States Foreign Policy and Operations*. Report prepared by Allen J. Ellender. 87th Cong., 2d sess., 1962. Senate Print 73.

_____. Senate. Committee on Foreign Relations. *The U.S. Government and the Vietnam War: Executive and Legislative Roles and Relationships Part I 1945-1961*. Report prepared by William Conrad Gibbons. 98th Cong., 2d sess., 1984. Senate Print 98-185.

_____. Senate. Committee on Foreign Relations. *The U.S. Government and the Vietnam War: Executive and Legislative Roles and Relationships, Part II, 1961-1964*. Report prepared by William Conrad Gibbons. 98th Cong., 2d sess., 1984. Senate Print 98-185.

_____. Senate. Charles Collingwood. 16 February 1971. [Television transcript]. "The Changing War in Indochina: The Widening War in Laos and Cambodia." CBS Television Network. *Congressional Record*, S2167-S2171 (1 March 1971).

Vongsavanh, Brigadier General Soutchay, *RLG Military Operations and Activities in the Laotian Panhandle*. Washington, D.C.: Center of Military History, 1981.

Secondary Sources

Andrade, Dale. "The War in Laos." *Armed Forces and Society* 22 (Summer 1996): 643-48.

Blaufarb, Douglas S. *Organizing and Managing Unconventional War in Laos*. R-919-ARPA. Santa Monica, Calif: Rand, 1972.

Burchett, Wilfred G. *The Second Indochina War: Cambodia and Laos.* New York: International Publishers, 1970.

Castle, Timothy N. *At War in the Shadow of Vietnam: U.S. Military Aid to the Royal Lao Government, 1955-1975.* New York: Columbia University Press, 1993.

Czyzak, John J., and Carl F. Salans. "The International Conference on the Settlement of the Laotian Question and the Geneva Agreements of 1962." *American Journal of International Law* 57 (April 1963): 300-17.

Dommen, Arthur J. *Conflict in Laos: The Politics of Neutralization.* New York: Praeger Publishers, 1971.

_____. "Laos: The Year of the Ho Chi Minh Trail." *Asian Survey* 12 (February 1972): 138-47.

_____. "Toward Negotiations in Laos." *Asian Survey* 11 (January 1971): 41-50.

Freeman, Nick. "Fighting the 'Non-Attributable War' in Laos: A Review Article." *Contemporary Southeast Asia* 17 (April 1996): 430-42.

Friedman, Edward, and Mark Seldon, eds. *American's Asia: Dissenting Essays on Asian-American Relations.* New York: Pantheon Books, 1969.

George, Alexander L., David K. Hall, and William E. Simons. *The Limits of Coercive Diplomacy: Laos, Cuba, Vietnam.* Boston, Mass.: Little, Brown, and Company, 1971.

_____., Philip J. Farley, and Alexander Dallin. *U.S.-Soviet Security Cooperation: Achievements, Failures, Lessons.* New York: Oxford University Press, 1988.

Goldstein, Martin E. *American Policy Toward Laos.* Cranbury, N.J.: Associated University Pressed, 1973.

Greenstein, Fred I., and Richard H. Immerman. "What Did Eisenhower Tell Kennedy about Indochina? The Politics of Misperception." *Journal of American History* 79 (September 1992): 568-87.

Gross, Leo. "The Question of Laos and the Double Veto in the Security Council." *American Journal of International Law* 54 (January 1960): 118-31.

Halpern, Barbara, and Joel Halpern. "Laos and America." *South Atlantic Quarterly* 63 (Spring 1964): 175-87.

Hammer, Ellen J. *The Struggle for Indochina.* Stanford, Calif.: Stanford University Press, 1954.

Healey, Denis. "Danger and Hope in Laos." *Eastern World* 15 (1961): 13.

"How Neutral is Laos?" *Intelligence Digest* 25 (June 1962): 14.
Hill, Kenneth L. "President Kennedy and the Neutralization of Laos." *Review of Politics* 31 (July 1969): 353-69.

Kerr, Allen D. "Municipal Government in Laos." *Asian Survey* 12 (June 1972): 510-17.

Kirk, Donald. *Wider War: The Struggle for Cambodia, Thailand, and Laos.* New York: Praeger, 1971.

Kochavi, Noam. "Limited Accommodation, Perpetuated Conflict: Kennedy, China, and the Laos Crisis, 1961-1963." *Diplomatic History* 26 (Winter 2002): 95-135.

Langer, Paul F., and Joseph J. Zasloff. *The North Vietnamese Military Adviser in Laos: A First Hand Account.* Santa Monica, Calif.: Rand, 1968.

_____. *North Vietnam and the Pathet Lao: Partners in the Struggle for Laos.* Cambridge, Mass.: Harvard University Press, 1970.

Leary, William M. "CIA Air Operations in Laos, 1955-1974." *Studies in Intelligence* 43 (Winter 1999-2000): 71-86.

_____. "The CIA and the 'Secret War' in Laos: The Battle for Skyline Ridge, 1971-1972." *Journal of Military History* 59 (July 1995): 507-17.

Lemmer, George F. *The Laos Crisis of 1959.* Christiansburg, Va.: Dalley Book Service, 1961.

Lee, Chae-Jin. "Communist China and the Geneva Conference on Laos: A Reappraisal." *Asian Survey* 9 (July 1969): 522-39.

Mahajani, Usha. "John Kennedy and United States Policy in Laos: 1961-1963." *Journal of Southeast Asian Studies* 2 (March 1971): 87-89.

Paul, Roland A. "Laos: Anatomy of an American Involvement." *Foreign Affairs* 49 (April 1971): 533-47

Pratt, Maj. John C. *The Royal Laotian Air Force: 1954-1970.* Christiansburg, Va.: Dalley Book Service, 1994.

Randle, Robert F. *Geneva 1954: The Settlement of the Indochinese War.* Princeton, N.J.: Princeton University Press, 1969.

Shaw, Geoffrey D. T. "Laotian 'Neutrality': A Fresh New Look at a Key Vietnam War Blunder." *Small Wars and Insurgencies* 13 (Spring 2002): 25-56.

Staaveren, Jacob Van. *Interdiction in Southern Laos: 1960-1968.* Washington, D.C.: Center for Air Force History, 1993.

Stanton, Thomas H. "Conflict in Laos: The Village Point of View." *Asian Survey* 8 (November 1968): 887-900.

Stevenson, Charles A. The End of Nowhere: *American Policy Towards Laos Since 1954.* Boston, Mass.: Beacon Press, 1972.

Toye, Hugh. *Laos: Buffer State or Battleground.* London: Oxford University Press, 1968.

"War in Laos." *Intelligence Digest* 26 (June 1963): 7.

Warner, Roger. *Back Fire: The CIA's Secret War in Laos and its Link to the War in Vietnam.* New York: Simon & Schuster, 1995.

White, Nick. "Macmillan, Kennedy and the Key West Meeting: Its Significance for the Laotian Civil War and Anglo-American Relations." *Civil Wars* 2 (Summer 1999): 35-55.

Wise, David, and Thomas B. Ross. *The Invisible Government.* New York: Random House, 1964.

Zasloff, Joseph J. *The Pathet Lao: Leadership and Organization.* Lexington, Mass.: Lexington Books, 1973.

Fig. 1. Political map of Laos

Table A1. The names and affiliations of key figures during the
Laotian crisis in the fall of 1960 (in order of appearance)

Name	Title	Affiliation	Description
Phoumi Nosavan	General/Minister of Defense	Rightist pro-Western anti-Communist	Refused to compromise with the Neutralist and eventually overthrew the Neutralist government
Kong Le	Captain/ Deputy Commander-in-Chief	Neutralist	Successfully overthrew Tiao Samsanith Rightist government
Souvanna Phouma	Prince/Prime Minister	Neutralist	Prime Minister (1951-1952, 1956-1957, and 1960) who attempted to form a neutral, coalition government in Laos
Sisavang Vong	King	none	Limited King who solicited United States aid to Laos and whose death sparked the rise of General Phoumi
Savang Vathana	King	none	Took a more active role in politics and attempted to negotiate a neutral, coalition government
Phoui Sananikone	Prime Minister	Neutralist pro-Western anti-Communist	The former Prime Minister who the United States advocated for Prime Minister in the fall of 1960 to establish a neutral government that favored the West.

Kou Abhay	Prime Minister	Rightist pro-Western anti-Communist	Set up the up a provisional government in spring of 1960.
Tiao Samsanith	Prime Minister	Rightist pro-Western anti-Communist	Fraudulently elected and a puppet for General Phoumi Nosavan
Christian Herter	Secretary of State	United States	Vacillated policies in order to settle the conflict, but actually prolonged the conflict.
Winthrop G. Brown	Ambassador	United States	The new ambassador who communicated with Laotian leaders regularly and relayed information back to the Secretary of State.
Ouane Rathikone	General	Neutralist, but shifted to Rightist	Appointed Commander in Chief of the Laotian forces by Prime Minister Souvanna and later defected to General Phoumi's side
Bounleth	General	Rightist pro-Western anti-Communist	Replaced Captain Kong Le as Deputy Chief of Staff
Amkha Soukhavong	General	Rightist pro-Western anti-Communist	Replaced Captain Kong Le as Deputy Commander-in-Chief

Boun Oum	Prince/Prime Minister	Rightist pro-Western anti-Communist	Became Prime Minister after the coup in December 1960
J. Graham Parsons	Assistant Secretary of State of East Asian and Pacific Affairs	United States	Inspected General Phoumi's forces and advocated for the cessation of aid to the Rightist
John N. Irwin II	Assistant Secretary of Defense	United States	Heard of General Phoumi's plan to take Vientiane in October, but told General Phoumi to wait
Herbert D. Riley	Vice Admiral	United States	Heard of General Phoumi's plan to take Vientiane in October, but told General Phoumi to wait
Baunpheun Isixiengmay	Major	Neutralist, but shifted to Rightist	Commander of the garrison in Luang Prabang who defected from Prime Minister Souvanna's forces and joined General Phoumi
Souphanouvong	Prince	Leftist Communist Pathet Lao	Half brother of Souvanna Phouma who was the leader of the Communist Pathet Lao organization
Kouprasith Abhay	Colonel	Neutralist, but shifted to Rightist	Helped General Phoumi carry out the invasion of Vientiane from the inside by deceiving Prime Minister Souvanna.
Quinim Polsena	Prime Minister/Minister of Information	Leftist	Became Prime Minister for a day when Prince Souvanna fled to Cambodia

Table A2. The names and affiliations of organizations during the Laotian crisis in the fall of 1960 (in order of appearance)

Name	Affiliations	Description
Pathet Lao	Leftist Communist	Name means "country of Laos," but it was the Communist organization in active rebellion against the Royal Laotian Government
Programs Evaluations Office	United States	A military headquarters for the United States in Laos disguised as an aid organization
National Assembly	Laotian government	The legislative body composed usually of about forty-one members
Royal Laotian Government	Laotian government	The entire Laotian government
Executive Committee of the High Command of the Revolution	Neutralist	Kong Le's council to reorganize the Royal Laotian Government
Forces Armee Lao	Laotian government	The Laotian military
Committee Against the Revolutionary Camp	Rightist anti-Communist pro-Western	General Phoumi Nosavan's council to organize a rebellion against the Neutralist controlled government
Neo Lao Hak Sat	Leftist Communist	The political party of the Pathet Lao
National Neutrality and Unity Committee	Neutralist	Council organized by Souvanna Phouma with Kong Le to establish a coalition government

www.ingramcontent.com/pod-product-compliance
Lightning Source LLC
Chambersburg PA
CBHW061233280526
45784CB00006B/2747